Chanekka Pullens Publishing Presents

Still Standing

Barbara Swint

Contact Information:

Email: imstillstandingllc@gmail.com

Still Standing

© 2021

Barbara Swint. All Rights Reserved.

Edited by Chanekka Pullens

No part of this book may be reproduced or transmitted in any form or by any means, written, electronic, recording, photocopying, or otherwise, without prior written permission of the author, Barbara Swint.

The names of individuals have been changed to protect the privacy of those involved.

Books may be purchased in quantity and/or special sales by contacting the author by email at: imstillstandingllc@gmail.com , with 'Book Purchase' in the subject line.

ISBN: 978-1-7355910-2-5

1. Autobiography 2.Christian 3. Inspiration

Printed in the USA

Dedication

I would like to dedicate this book to my one and only child, my gift from God, Chriseanthea Flowers. This book is also dedicated to all the survivors of sexual abuse and to all the children who are born from sexual abuse.

Psalm 139:14

"I praise you because I am fearfully and wonderfully made; your works are wonderful. I know that full well."

Acknowledgements

I would like to thank God for giving me the courage to write this book. I also would like to acknowledge my childhood friend, Tashawlia Pinkney, for being there for me when I was at my lowest. Your words of encouragement gave me a reason to keep fighting. May you rest in love, my friend. And a special thank you to Tracie Bailey for bringing my vision to life.

Letter to My Younger Self

Dear Five-year-old Me,

May I just say, "thank you" to the little girl that I was. Thank you for all you went through to allow me to be the woman I am today. I am so thankful to God that you survived, even when I didn't want to. Your pureness and strength ushered me here. Thank you for these forty-five years. I love you. We made it!

-Love Barbara

Table of Contents

Home……………………………………………………………..1

Death of Innocence……………………………………………..8

Life Changes……………………………………………………14

The Aftermath………………………………………………….20

The Footprint Years……………………………………………25

The Shift…………………………………………………………28

Closure……………………………………………………………31

Still Standing……………………………………………………38

Sexual Abuse Terms and Statistics…………………………41

Tips for Handling Sexual Assault/Abuse………………….44

Scriptures………………………………………………………..45

Home

I was born on August 20, 1975 to Delores and James Davis. I was their only child although I had several siblings. My mom had three older sons from her first marriage that lived with their dad. My dad had three daughters and two sons. My parents were hardworking and well known in our small Florida town. My mom cleaned houses and worked at a restaurant to make a living. My dad worked at a local lumber company. He spent his free time singing in a gospel group, The Harmoneers. He sang in a smooth, bass voice that reminded me of Melvin Franklin from The Temptations. His group traveled all over the South. They even made an album and appeared on tv.

When I was born, my parents brought me home to our little wooden house. This is where we lived until I was six years old. Although it was more like a shack, it was our home. There was a kitchen, living room, bathroom, and two small bedrooms. I mostly remember the kitchen where the floor had a hole in it from where the wood had rotted. I remember falling through that hole so many times and ending up under the house! We did not have a lot of money, but I was happy because at least I had my dad in our home with us.

Although I had a great relationship with both of my parents, I was definitely a daddy's girl. No matter what I did, he always let me get away with it. I remember the time in kindergarten when I decided to cut my hair off. I came home and told my mom that one of my classmates had done it. I was relieved when she believed me. I was so glad that I had gotten away with it. However, that victory came to an end when I looked out of the window and saw my teacher walking up to our front door. I nervously listened as my teacher explained to my parents that I had cut my hair off at school. After she left, my mom ordered me to prepare for an old-fashioned whooping.

Thankfully, my dad intervened and came to my rescue as usual. "Leave her alone. It'll grow back", he laughed.

Although we had some good times, there were also some dark times. My parents had begun to argue a lot because of my dad's drinking. When he drank, he became someone else. It was like Dr. Jekyll and Mr. Hyde. He would quickly change from one demeanor to another. My mom would usually be the one on the receiving end of his anger. It didn't take much to set him off. One time, he got mad at her over what she had cooked for dinner. She fixed his plate and sat it on the table in front of him.

He scowled as he looked the food over. "I don't want this mess!", he shouted as he picked the plate up and hurled it against the wall. He then ordered my mom to clean up the mess he had made, and she quickly obliged.

When my parents fought, I would become so fearful and nervous from all the noise. I would sit in my room, biting my nails until they bled. Watching the way my mother was treated taught me at a young age to be a people pleaser. I believed that the best way to avoid getting beaten and yelled at in relationships was to do what the other person wanted.

This is called fawning. Fawning is defined as the use of people pleasing to diffuse conflict, feel more secure in relationships, and earn the approval of others. The person displaying this behavior basically behaves in a way that he or she feels will be acceptable to others and keep them safe from conflict or abuse. People that fawn tend to put themselves last in order to make sure the needs of others are met. There are no boundaries in one's relationships when the person is a people pleaser. This behavior can be found, most times, in those that experienced growing up in dysfunctional and abusive environments. Fawning can be a physical, mental, and emotional response to trauma.

All of the constant fighting finally led to my parents breaking up when I was six years old. Even though I was young, I was devastated when my parents went their separate ways. Divorce can be as stressful for children as it is for the parents. That kind of stress is even harder for children that have been exposed to toxic environments.

Sadly, my dad wasn't in my life much after he split from my mom. It is as if he decided to end his relationship with me as well as her. I rarely saw or talked to him after that. It wasn't until I was grown that we started trying to repair our father/daughter relationship. We started talking more, and I would also go visit him whenever I was in town. I am so grateful that we had the chance to get things right before he passed.

When he left, I was both hurt and relieved. Although he and my mom fought constantly, his presence always made me feel safe. I know that if he knew about the things that I would end up suffering at the hands of abusers, he would have killed someone. I remember once my cousin and I had an incident when I was five. We were playing outside when he picked up a rock and threw it. The rock hit me in the head so hard, I still have a bump on my head to this day.

I ran into the house crying to my aunt. "Don't tell your dad," she told me as she tried to calm me down. Even though it was an accident, my aunt knew that my dad did not play when it came to me. He was a highly respected man whose presence could put the fear of God in you.

The relief of his leaving came because I knew no matter how good he treated me, my mom was experiencing the total opposite. It was so bad that my aunt, my dad's sister, warned my mother to leave before he ended up killing her. It was a very unhealthy and toxic environment for me to see and hear fights almost daily. I was happy for her to have the courage to leave him because this was not her first abusive relationship. Prior to him, she had been in several abusive relationships. She was also sexually abused as a child. When she was fourteen, my mom was married off to a grown man to cover up the fact that she was violated by him.

By the time she was seventeen, she had three children by this man. She later found the strength to leave him, but she still had not healed from the wounds and trauma of that relationship.

Both of my parents were dealing with their own demons which caused problems in their relationship. My dad had not healed from losing his mother at the age of twelve. I believe that was the root cause of his anger. He later turned to alcohol to ease his pain. However, pain and alcohol were not a good combination for him.

I learned from my parents the true meaning of "hurt people hurt people". It's not always intentional, but that is what happens when there is no proper help or guidance. To this day, I still love both of my parents dearly and unconditionally despite their flaws. If I could talk to them today, I would tell my mom, "I love you. I get it and now, I have received my healing. I have broken the generational curses attached to our lineage." I would tell my dad, "I love you and I will forever be a daddy's girl."

They are among the reasons why I decided to share my story. It is time for families to overcome fear and shame in order to tell, expose, and confront the things that have been swept under the carpet for generations.

Generational curses are sins, beliefs, and patterns that are passed down from generation to generation in a lineage. There are different types of behaviors that affect families. In some families, marriages commonly end in divorce. In others, there are various kinds of abuse and/or addiction. Some families even suffer from poverty, gluttony, or not being able to reach their full potential. Although these things can cause chains to tightly grip a family, I know for myself that God can break every chain into pieces. Nothing is too hard for Him. I don't care how long something has had someone in bondage, God can heal and deliver. He set me free from years of hurt and trauma. He brought light where there had only been darkness. I decided to tell my story so that others can know that what God did for me, he can surely do for them.

Death of Innocence

I remember the day my life was turned upside down. I was just four years old. By this time, my sixteen-year-old brother, Greg, had moved in with us due to his dad physically abusing him. On this particular day, my mom had to go to town to pick up some things from the store. She didn't want to wake me, so she decided to leave me with Greg. She left him with instructions to send me to my Aunt Lanette's house right down the road from us when I woke up. When I finally woke up, he told me what my mom had said.

I got ready and was just about to walk out of the door when I heard my brother call me. "Barbara! Come here a minute," he called.

Although I didn't know my brother well, I had no reason to fear him. So, I went back to see what he wanted. When I got to his room, he ordered me to sit on the bed. I did as he asked and obeyed. Then, he asked me to lay down. The next thing I knew, he had pinned me under him. I squirmed as he tried to place his penis into my vagina. He was very forceful, and it hurt very badly. I didn't understand what was happening, but something inside of me told me that what he was doing was wrong. After what felt like an eternity, he rose off of me and stood up.

"You better not tell mom, or I'll do it again," he threatened as he zipped his pants up and buttoned them.

"I won't tell," I promised.

I jumped up and quickly ran out of the door holding my stomach because of the pain. I ran all the way to my aunt's house. When I got there, I laid down on her couch and held my private area as I tried to catch my breath. I couldn't believe the pain my brother had caused me. The pain penetrated my body, my mind, and my heart. It was all so overwhelming.

"Why didn't mom just take me with her," I wondered to myself as tears streamed down my face.

The situation was too much for my young body and mind to handle. I laid there and cried until I fell asleep. When my mom came to pick me up, I wanted so badly to tell her what had happened. As soon as I was about to tell her what happened to me, I remembered my brother's threat and the menacing look in his eyes. I remembered the fear that I felt as I struggled to break free from the hold he had on my arms. I then decided to keep quiet because I never wanted to feel that pain again. I felt like my brother would make good on his threat. From that point, my mind blocked out the trauma my body had experienced. It was years before those memories would resurface.

After the incident with Greg, life continued as usual. However, I wasn't the same little girl that I was before. Before that, I was a happy go lucky child. I was shy, had low self-esteem, and I didn't trust authority. I withdrew myself from the world. From that day forward, I was a shell of my old self; just going through the motions.

My speech was also affected by what happened. It got so bad, that when I started kindergarten, I had to go to speech therapy because I had trouble pronouncing words. I later read that trauma can affect your speech. In some cases, it can take away your ability to speak altogether. The National Child Traumatic Stress Network states that children who have experienced complex trauma often find it difficult to identify and manage their emotions. This can lead to having limited language for what one is feeling. That one incident changed the person that I was supposed to grow up to be.

Over the next five years, Greg behaved as if he had never done anything to me. He and I had never had a close relationship due to our age difference. We didn't behave as siblings towards each other. I felt that since I had kept what he did a secret, he wouldn't bother me anymore. I was so wrong.

One day, when I was eleven, I was playing in my room when I heard him call my name. I went to see what he wanted. I stepped into the room and found him and one of his friends listening to music. Suddenly, Greg jumped up from where he was sitting and grabbed me. Next, he pushed me down to the floor. I squirmed and struggled to get free from his grasp. It was a losing battle because he was bigger and stronger. He pinned me down by my arms as his friend began to touch me sexually. Then, he took his turn touching me. Finally, they let me up and I ran back to my room. I laid across my bed and cried until I couldn't cry anymore. I couldn't believe that my brother had violated me again. And to make it worse, he allowed someone else to do it as well.

I decided that when my mom got home, I would tell her that Greg had hurt me. I was nervous to tell, but I knew I had to say something. I just knew that she would step in and make him stop hurting me. When she got home, I told her that he had hurt me. I didn't give her any details about what happened; I just wanted her to know that he hurt me in some way. Unfortunately, she didn't do anything about it. I couldn't believe I was left to face the pain on my own. I felt so alone and helpless.

The trauma I experienced caused my mind to shut down which caused my body to shut down also. It was as if my mind and body were working together to protect my sanity. This was good in that I didn't lose my mind. However, many years passed before I could fully remember the details of the molestation. As a matter of fact, when the second incident happened, I didn't even remember that the first one occurred.

According to Dr. Muriel Salmona, complete or fragmented traumatic amnesia is a common memory disorder found in victims of violence. The mind literally cuts off a traumatic memory as the body goes into survival mode. These buried memories often resurface due to certain triggers. These triggers can be something you see, hear, taste, or smell. It might be meeting someone that reminds you of the person that caused the trauma by their appearance or the way they speak. It could be the smell of someone's perfume or cologne that brings a painful event back to remembrance.

Even though I didn't remember Greg molesting me, God put something in me that made me cautious around him. I made it a point to never be alone with him. When he was around me, the hairs on my arm would stand up. I always felt uneasy in his presence. I would get an unexplainable feeling in the pit of my stomach. If we both happened to be in the same room, I would hurry to grab what I needed, then run to my room where it was safe. I would lock the door just in case he tried to come in. It was pure hell to live like that every single day. This went on until I eventually moved out.

The worst incident involving Greg happened when I was twelve. I was in my bed sound asleep when I suddenly woke up to find him on top of me. Immediately, I yelled for my mom. She was on the opposite side of the house and couldn't hear me calling for help. That is when he pulled out a knife and threatened me. Fearing for my life, I laid there, shaking like a leaf as I let him do whatever he wanted to do to me. Afterwards, I wanted to go to the bathroom and clean up but, my body wouldn't cooperate. It was as if I had totally shut down. As I lay there trembling, I prayed to God to take it away because it was too much to deal with. Instantly, I felt calm and drifted off to sleep. The next morning at breakfast, my stepdad asked if I was yelling the night before. I shook my head as I wondered if he dreamt that I screamed. Because of the trauma, I had no memory of the previous night. It was all totally erased.

Life Changes

The next person to sexually abuse me was my aunt's boyfriend. This is the incident of assault that would change my life forever.

The first time I met him was at my Aunt Wanda's house. I walked into her house and found her talking to a man.

"George, this is my niece, Barbara," Aunt Wanda introduced.

"Hello," he smiled.

"Hello," I replied politely.

After the introduction, I left to go home. I didn't want to disturb my aunt while she had company.

The next time I saw George was one Sunday morning. I stopped by Aunt Wanda's house on the way to church. When I walked in, he was there. While we had small talk, I mentioned that I was on my way to church. He reached into his pocket and pulled out some folded bills.

"Put this in church," he said as he handed me the money.

"Thank you," I said as I took the money from his hand.

After that day, he began to get closer to the family. He was especially close to the kids. As a kid, I loved to skate, but my mom wouldn't let me go unsupervised. So, Aunt Wanda and George would take us. He would put on skates and get out on the floor with us. We all would have such a good time. I know now that he was grooming me through kindness to get me to be comfortable around him.

Grooming is a process that sexual predators use to gain a person's trust over time in order to eventually sexually abuse them. Pedophiles often seek situations where there is access to children. This can happen at school, church, or through a romantic relationship with someone that has children. They might target one child or several. From there, they will form a bond.

They might do that through compliments, common interests, gift giving, etc. It's a form of manipulation to get someone to let their guard down and trust them.

One night, George decided to make his move. It happened when I spent the night at my aunt's house. Later that night, I fell asleep on the floor. When she went to take a shower, he came over to me and tried to pull my legs apart. I was horrified when I realized he was trying to remove my panties. His attempt was unsuccessful. He gave up once he heard my aunt turn the water off in the shower. He never told me not to tell, but in my subconscious, I knew from previous experience not to say anything or it could happen again.

One day in July when I was thirteen, my mom told me to go to my aunt's house. I was glad to go because I did not want to be alone with my brother. When I got there, Aunt Wanda was not home. George was there though, and my cousins were in the other room asleep.

George and I were sitting on the couch together. He suddenly put his hand over my mouth, pushed me back on the couch, and violated me. I felt so alone and confused.

"Why does this keep happening? Is something wrong with me?" I thought as I tried to disconnect myself from what was happening. I laid there feeling helpless as this grown man destroyed what was left of my innocence.

Sometime after that, he asked me if I've had sex before. I told him no and that I was a virgin. I guess he was trying to cover his tracks in case something came up. He also kept asking if I had come on my cycle yet, in which I told him that I had not. I really did not understand why he was asking me these things. Soon after, he stopped coming around.

On September 30, 1989, I realized why he suddenly disappeared. I found out what he already knew. I was pregnant. And I was only fourteen years old.

My mom had always kept up with my cycle. When it stopped, she took me to the doctor. He confirmed that I was pregnant. She and one of my aunts began to question me about who I had been having sex with. I didn't have an answer for them because I was totally in shock. There I was a baby about to have a baby. At this time, I didn't even know how babies were made because my mom had never given me the birds and the bees talk. I knew I should tell my mom about Aunt Wanda's boyfriend being the cause of the situation.

However, I just couldn't find the words, so, I decided to write her a letter instead. I told her everything that had transpired. After reading the letter, my mom took me to the police station. A detective recorded me as I recounted the details of my story. Unfortunately, things went the same way as the first time I tried to tell someone about being assaulted. Nothing was done. Nevertheless, I didn't see George again.

Pregnancy was really hard for me. Although I didn't have morning sickness or complications, it was emotionally stressful. I was so young and overwhelmed with how my body was changing to accommodate the new life inside of me. It was also hard to deal with the stares and whispers of peers and family members. Since I lived in a small town, news of my condition traveled fast. It was especially hurtful to overhear family members gossiping about me. At least my friends had enough decency not to ask me questions about my pregnancy.

One of my biggest supporters was a friend that I had known since kindergarten. She really stepped up when I needed someone to be in my corner. Even though we were teenagers, she was very wise for her age. She was so caring and encouraging, and her support meant so much to me.

Eventually, I had to withdraw from regular school because of my pregnancy. I was sent to an alternative school for my 8th grade year. At first, it was a breath of fresh air because my main friends who knew what had happened to me, were not there. Then, it sank in what going to the alternative school really meant for me. Going there meant no dances or sports; there were only core classes. I felt as if I was in a fog as I slowly saw my childhood slip away. I became depressed as I watched my friends do normal things that I could no longer participate in. I kept asking God over and over why this was happening to me. I now know that God had a plan and purpose for me and for my child. My baby had a destiny no matter how she was conceived. After that realization, I finally accepted that the child I used to be was now gone forever as I was forced into a life of adult responsibilities.

The Aftermath

I went on to have a healthy pregnancy without any complications. Finally, on April 16, 1990, I gave birth to a baby girl at the age of fourteen. Although I loved my daughter more than anything, I couldn't shake the depression that had taken over my life. I was also suffering from PTSD.

Post-Traumatic Stress Disorder (PTSD). It is often associated with those that have served in the military. PTSD is defined as a psychiatric disorder that can occur in people who has experienced or witnessed a traumatic event such as a natural disaster, a serious accident, a terrorist act, war/combat, rape, the threat of death, or serious injury. However, studies have shown that victims of sexual abuse or assault can experience the same struggle with trauma. After sexual assault, feelings of shame, guilt, anxiety, fear, anger, and sadness are common in survivors. These feelings can continue for months or years and effect every part of the person's life. In addition, PTSD can develop and cause trust issues and/or nightmares.

Being sexually abused affected me in every area of my life. I struggled academically which eventually caused me to drop out of school. I was already going through so much in my home life, I was not able to focus. After a while, I got so frustrated that I quit. It took me years to go back.

Another major way the abuse affected me was in my self-esteem. I didn't have a healthy view of myself which caused me to let others treat me in a way that was less than I deserved. I also couldn't properly express myself and my feelings. I would bottle things up on the inside until I exploded. According to the Children's Traumatic Stress Network, children who have experienced complex trauma often have difficulty identifying, expressing, and managing emotions. They often internalize or externalize stress reactions that result in depression, anxiety, or anger.

Internalizing my feelings caused me to act out in other ways. I coped by smoking marijuana and became hypersexual. I developed low self-esteem and was unable to see my true worth.

I had major trust issues that affected all of my relationships. I didn't trust any man that said they loved me. I wasn't faithful to anyone because of my distrust. I also developed a distrust of my mother and other adults because I felt like no one came to my rescue when I needed help. I had trouble relating to my peers which made me feel like I had nowhere to turn. I felt as if I was all alone in the world.

My issues also impacted my relationship with my daughter. I was there physically for her, but not emotionally. It was almost like an out of body experience as I went through the motions of caring for her. I made sure she bathed, ate, etc. However, I couldn't properly express my love. I definitely loved my daughter, but I had a hard time expressing something to her that was never expressed to me. At the end of the day, I was still a child trying to raise a child without being whole or healed. As she grew into a teenager, my trauma began to show up in her. It came out in the way she acted out and in our disagreements. We lived in pure dysfunction until I decided to get healed from the trauma of my childhood.

When I was fifteen, I met someone that would change my life forever and for the better. I met a guy named Mike. He was five years older than me, and I immediately realized he was different from the other guys that I was used to dealing with. He didn't try to do anything sexual with me and he treated me with respect. I felt that maybe it was because I was underage. But that didn't stop others from trying.

We were friends for a short time. He even took a liking to my daughter who was four months old then. He was such a good guy. Eventually, I became overwhelmed by being treated so nice by him and I ended our friendship. I was too broken to even accept his kindness. He seemed too good to be true.

A couple of years later, I ran into Mike again around town. He informed me that he was at home on leave from the military. Next, he invited me to go to the movies with him. Then, he asked my mom for permission to take me out. I was so happy when she said yes. It was at that moment that I knew he was different from the rest. We ended up hanging out the entire time that he was home. It was definitely a whirlwind romance the way that everything progressed so quickly. The next thing I knew, I was in love. For the first time, I knew what true love was. I had never had a guy treat me so good. More than anything, I felt safe and comfortable with him. When his leave was over, I gave him my address so that we could keep in touch. We wrote and talked every chance that we got.

On March 19, 1994, I married Mike, the love of my life. We had a small house wedding. The guest list included my mom, stepdad, my best friend, and her cousin. My pastor married us. At the time, we did not have a lot of money. We were not even able to afford a honeymoon. However, we were not going to let that stop us from being together. Our love was enough to take us through anything we faced. We were young but we were truly in love. He was the man of my dreams and my best friend. He also loved my daughter like his own. Although this was the happiest time of my life, I was still dealing with the effects of my childhood traumas.

At this point, Mike didn't know about any of the abuse that I had suffered. I wasn't able to talk about it, mainly because I wasn't ready to face it myself. The other part was the fact that I had repressed memories about some of the things that had taken place because of the trauma. What I didn't realize then was that I was not going to get healed from my wounds until I gave everything over to God.

The Footprint Years

I named this chapter "The Footprint Years" based on the poem, *Footprints in the Sand*. The narrator in the poem explains that while looking back over his life with God, he noticed two sets of footprints in some places and one set in other places. The person noticed that it was only one set of footprints in the lowest point of his life. God explained that it was during those times that He carried him. I call the years between my marriage and my healing from God "Footprint Years" because He truly carried me when I was going through my lowest point. I was totally engulfed in my trauma from the events surrounding my daughter's conception and the aftermath.

After Mike and I got married, we moved to Virginia. Since I was from a small town, moving to a big city was quite different for me. For one, I didn't know anybody there except for one cousin. I was happy to get the chance to start over in a new place. It was like a breath of fresh air. However, I didn't realize I was bringing my dysfunction with me to my new home.

My trauma eventually started to emerge in the form of a reckless lifestyle. I was drinking, partying, and doing whatever my heart desired. For many years, I lived this way, I didn't have a care in the world. I believe in a way that I was trying to recapture my stolen childhood. When other kids my age were partying and running the streets, I was home raising my daughter. My mother was very strict, so I couldn't do anything anyway. I looked at Virginia as an opportunity to, for once, do what I wanted and feel like I had some sort of control over my own life. It is said that hurt people hurt people. I mostly hurt myself though as I continued to internalize my pain. I was so mentally tired, that I didn't care if I lived or died. I was tired of guilt, shame, brokenness, etc. I wanted to be whole! I wanted to be free!

During this time, I was still a wife and a mother. However, I did the bare minimum. I made sure my daughter had her physical needs met. But, when it came to her emotional needs, I dropped the ball. Deep down, I knew I wanted to do better for my family. I just didn't know how.

One thing that didn't change was church. No matter where I was or what I was going through, I always found a church to go to. Through it all, I knew God had a plan and purpose for my life.

I came from a very religious family. We were a typical Black Southern Baptist family. We regularly attended and served in our church. My dad sang in the male chorus, our local community choir, and the gospel group. I too sang in the kid's choir.

God has always been a big part of my life. He was the rock that I leaned on when things got rough. He was the one that brought me through to the other side when I couldn't get past my pain.

The Shift

One day in 2010, God started talking to me about fully giving my life to Him. He said that He had so much that He wanted to do for me. He wanted to heal me of all the trauma and dysfunction of my past in order to bring me to a place of forgiveness.

That Sunday, I visited a church. I was so moved by the service that I ended up joining. When there was a call to the altar, I stood up from my seat and made my way down to the front. I went to the altar and gave my life completely to Christ that day. At that very moment, my life was changed. I felt like a new person. I knew that the old Barbara was gone, and that God had given me a new life. Soon after that, I was baptized, and God gave me His precious Holy Spirit. He knew I needed His Spirit to lead and guide me through what was to come.

In October of 2012, I traveled to Atlanta, GA to attend the Woman Thou Art Loosed Conference. It changed my life! The conference was hosted by Bishop TD Jakes; every year he chooses a different theme. That year, the theme was "You Have it in You: Empowered to Do the Impossible". This theme really struck a chord in my spirit. I had learned about God's Holy Spirit that lives on the inside of believers. I knew that the Holy Spirit brought power. That meant that the power that I needed in order to do what seemed impossible was already there inside of me. I got excited thinking about the freedom that could be mine because of God's power in me!

For three days, I experienced things I never had before. I worshipped with people from various denominations and nationalities. It felt like what heaven must feel like. We were all there together for one reason only - to worship the true and living God. God's power was so strong in the room.

On the last night of the conference, I decided I was leaving there free. That night, Tasha Cobbs was the musical guest. She was leading praise and worship. As she began to sing, "Break Every Chain", I began to worship God in spirit and in truth. It was what I imagined the day of Pentecost was like. Everybody was there on one accord, and the power of the Holy Spirit hit that place.

So, I decided that I was leaving there free. I knew it was a now or never moment. I knew that my healing was in the room that night because God's Spirit lives in me. I was ready to completely let go and receive the healing that I knew only God could give. I lifted my eyes towards heaven and opened my mouth to let the cry loose that was building up in me. A worship came forth from my belly to my mouth that was like a river of flowing water. I began to cry out as my mouth filled with my heavenly language. Right in the middle of all of those people, I cried out like I never had before. Suddenly, I could feel the heavy chains literally breaking. The chains that had been as heavy as bricks were falling off! I started to feel lighter and lighter as if I were floating above my seat.

I now know that I was experiencing the power of God and getting to know Him for myself. I worshipped God in my brokenness, and He gave me freedom and peace in return. I had peace in my mind. Peace in my spirit. Peace in my heart. I was experiencing the perfect peace that surpasses understanding that the Bible talks about. I felt hurt, pain, shame, guilt, and unforgiveness fall away from me. I began to praise God and thank Him in my heavenly language. For the first time in my life, I was free, healed, and spiritually full. I now know that through Him, what seems impossible becomes possible. I vowed that from that day forward, I would always give His name the praise for keeping me and bringing me through. With a grateful heart, I say to God be all the glory!

I left that conference and went home a changed woman. I returned and continued to grow in the Lord. By December of that year, God opened a door that was closed for twenty-two years. I got the chance to talk to my abuser who was also my daughter's father.

Closure

After I left the Woman Thou Art Loosed Conference in October, I came home and partnered with Bishop T. D. Jakes' ministry. I wanted to be a blessing to his ministry since my healing had come through God using his ministry. When I came home, I felt so free and peaceful. I am so glad that I was in a better place overall to be able to face what was coming up.

One day in December of 2012, I was casually scrolling through Facebook as I often did. As I was laughing at funny posts and looking at selfies, it came to my mind to search for the name of my daughter's biological father. I had tried to look for him a few times over the years, however, not knowing exactly where he was made it fairly impossible. I now know that everything happens in God's time. If God had allowed our paths to cross before I received my healing, I would have killed him!

So that day in December, I carefully typed his name into the search bar. I took a deep breath and hit the enter button. Instantly, his picture popped up. I was so shocked to see him after all the years that had passed. I panicked and quickly shut the computer down.

Two days later, I got up enough nerve to send him a friend request. I also sent him a message on Facebook

Messenger. I typed the message out and carefully reviewed it when I was finished. I chuckled to myself as I read it. I knew from the words that I wrote that God had saved me for real. The tone was nice nasty, but I didn't curse him out like the old me would have. It's amazing how God changes a person!

Imagine my surprise when he actually responded. I was completely shocked because I honestly didn't expect a response. In his message, he said that we needed to talk. He sent me his number so that I could call him. So, the time came to make one of the hardest phone calls of my life. I was so nervous as I dialed the number. When he answered, I told him who I was. I told him what he did to me and informed him that he had a daughter.

There was a pause as he opened his mouth and said something I couldn't believe he had the nerve to say. "I'll send you some child support," he responded.

"Hell, my daughter is grown!" I yelled out of frustration.

My daughter was twenty-two at the time and way passed needing child support. His response showed me how twisted the mind of a child molester can be. He then went on to tell me that he was in love with me when everything happened all those years ago. I was thirteen years old when he sexually abused me! He was a grown thirty-one-year-old man.

I decided then and there that I was not going to let anything he said make me mad. This conversation was not about him. It was all about me getting my feelings and emotions out. Before we ended the call, he surprisingly admitted to his wrongdoing. I just knew that he was going to lie about it. Although, I believe that he only admitted it because he felt that nothing could be done to him at that point because so much time had passed.

I didn't need an apology from him because I had already forgiven him. I just wanted him to know that he had a child who didn't ask to be here. My daughter had questions that only he could answer.

Someone that I knew from back home had told my daughter the truth about her conception while she was visiting relatives in my hometown. It was completely devastating when she found out the truth. I didn't know that she knew until one day she let it out. My daughter is like me in that way. She holds things in until they come out as an explosion. Our relationship was toxic for years after that.

After I said what I wanted and needed to say, I hung up. I never talked to him again after that phone call. I thanked God for opening that door. I was glad for the closure that conversation gave me so I could move on.

My healing continued over time. Before I could get total deliverance, the trauma that I had suppressed had to be brought back to my remembrance. As aforementioned, my mind blocked everything out because the abuse was so traumatic. At this time, I was so nervous and scared about remembering it all. I didn't know what I would do once I remembered everything. Honestly, I didn't think I was strong enough to handle it all. But I had to learn that you can't heal what you don't reveal.

The reason for my concern was the fact that mental illness is one of the generational curses that runs in my family. That's why I often thank God that through it all, He kept my mind. Without Him, I would have lost all functions of my being. I believe the reason He chose to reveal the memories over time, is because He knew my heart and concerns. That's how good God is! He will meet you right where you are. You don't have to pretend you have it all together. He works best with the broken pieces.

The first memory God revealed to me was when I was an innocent four-year-old girl being sexually abused by my brother. It shook me to my core. I felt sick thinking about my own brother doing something like that to me. Then, I realized that's the reason why I had always felt so wary and unsafe around him. My main question was why would he do this? At that time, I had so many questions and no answers. I thought about going to him about what I remembered. However, I decided it wasn't the best thing to do because at the time, my brother kept going in and out of the mental hospital. I decided to take the steps that were necessary for me to heal and move forward.

I first had to acknowledge that it happened. So many times, things like this remain hidden, unacknowledged, and swept under the rug. But a lot of people don't realize that denial will delay the healing.

Next, I came to a place of acceptance. I accepted that what happened was not my fault. I know I wasn't to blame for the unfortunate choices that my brother made. So many times, victims will feel guilty and blame themselves for the actions of others. Or others might try and make them feel guilty for what was done to them. Someone that has been sexually assaulted or abused might be told that they were asking for it by their behavior or attire. These things don't justify assault. There is no justification when there wasn't consent.

Lastly, I took time to grieve for my innocence that was stolen. Since I couldn't remember some of the things that were done to me, I wasn't able to fully comprehend how these things affected me as a child. I was able to do this after God healed me and revealed what happened to me. I also prayed daily for God to keep my sanity intact. He faithfully carried me through everything I faced just like He has all my life.

The last stage of my healing came in June 2017. I kept feeling like there was something else that God wanted to reveal to me. I felt nervous because I was in such a great place mentally, emotionally, and spiritually. God knew my heart, so He had to ease this one on me.

It happened when I visited my hometown like I had on many occasions. I stopped by the house of one of my sisters, Diane. We talked for a while, until there was a knock on her door. When she opened it, there was a guy standing there. He said that he was there to see my sister's boyfriend. She stepped back and let him in. Once I saw him, I had this nagging feeling that I knew him. He must have felt the same because he asked my sister's boyfriend who I was. He proceeded to tell him who I was and mentioned my brother.

"I remember when you were a little girl," he said with a look of recognition on his face. "Me and your brother were best friends in school. You don't remember, do you?"

Immediately, memories started to flash through my mind. My stomach dropped as I realized he was the guy that had a part in assaulting me. It all played out in my mind like a movie as the memories rushed back to me. I wanted to get up and leave, but I felt as if I were frozen in time. After some time, I left and went to my aunt's house where I was staying for my visit home. When I got inside, I staggered to the couch and collapsed. I just sat there and cried as I tried to process what had just happened. The tears flowed as I dealt with the realization that I had been sexually abused throughout my life by multiple men. These were men that I should have been able to trust.

After I cried, I decided to accept that it happened and released it. I had let go of the final piece of my past that was holding me back. I then started praising and thanking God for keeping me through the revelations and every day of my life. From that day forward, I have been set free and I'm no longer living in bondage to my past.

Still Standing

Now that I have been healed, I have decided to dedicate my life to helping others find healing and freedom from the effects of abuse. I received training to become a Crisis Intervention Counselor. I take calls and conduct assessments with clients to determine their specific needs. Some of the services include providing referrals for medical service, assistance, or psychiatric intervention if required. I am a Sexual Assault Advocate which is a personal liaison for recent sexual assault or domestic violence victims and their families. We also provide moral and emotional support. I really flourish in these assignments because these were things that I had experienced. I am able to relate to what our clients have been through.

This year, I officially started my own organization called Still Standing. Still Standing is a safe place for all sexual assault victims to come and share their story without judgement. Sometimes it is so hard for victims to share their experiences due to fear of judgement or backlash. I also provide a place where resources are available to those that need them.

The accomplishment that I am most proud of is receiving my high school diploma after dropping out years ago. I tried to go back to school after quitting, but

I wasn't focused. It always bothered me that I did not complete school. Once I had the chance to go back, I was determined not to quit no matter what. Sometimes it was a struggle, but I knew I had to finish what I started. The day that I received my diploma was one of the best days of my life. I did it for me, my family, and as a testament to others that you can do whatever you put your mind to with God's help. It is never too late to reach your goals.

I am enjoying living my God given purpose. I have been able to heal and embrace life after trauma and dysfunction. I am so in love with my new life! I tell my truth every chance I get. I share my story in hopes that others will be encouraged, inspired, and healed. I also take time out for self-care when I need it. I have learned to put myself first. That was hard for me at first because I'm a caregiver by nature. I always want to make sure others are okay and taken care of. Over the years, this left me drained and weighed down. It came down to choosing them or my sanity. I chose the latter. Every day, I do something special for myself. It might be a candlelit bubble bath, reading, taking a walk, praying, or one of my personal favorites - shopping. Retail therapy is helpful but can get costly! It helps to find hobbies and activities that bring you joy and allow you to treat yourself.

Another thing that can help is going to therapy. There is a huge taboo against seeking out help through a therapist in the black community. Many times, people are walking around broken and traumatized because they have been forced to sweep hurtful incidents under the rug. Many times, well-meaning parents and relatives will instruct children to do this because they themselves have experienced trauma. I have started therapy sessions and I am not ashamed about that. God is our healer, period. However, He uses natural means to help us as well. That may come in the form of seeking out professional help. Sometimes, we just need to talk things out with someone and get it all out of our system. Although God already healed me, going to therapy is a way to work through traits that I picked up during the years of dysfunction. I'm learning new ways of thinking so I can be my best.

Each day, I live my truth and thank God every step of the way. I often think back to different things that were a help to me during my healing process. One thing that really stands out is the song, "I'm Still Standing" by Marvin Sapp. That song ministered to me in some of my darkest moments. Now, light has replaced darkness. I feel light where I was heavy. Bondage has been replaced by freedom. No more chains are holding me! I thank God that because of Him and His love for me, I am still standing!

Sexual Abuse Terms and Statistics

The following statistics and definitions were published by the National Crime Victimization Survey (NCVS):

Rape - Forced sexual intercourse including both psychological coercion as well as physical force. Includes attempted rape. Attempted rape includes verbal threats of rape.

Sexual Assault - A wide range of victimizations, separate from rape or attempted rape. These crimes include attacks or attempted attacks generally involving unwanted sexual contact between victim and offender. Sexual assaults may or may not involve force and can include such things as grabbing or fondling. It also includes verbal threats.

Victim - Refers to someone who has been recently affected by sexual violence.

Survivor - Refers to someone who has gone through the recovery process.

1 in 3 girls and 1 in 5 boys experience sexual assault at the hands of an adult before the age of 18.

Effects can be long lasting and affect the victim's mental health.

Victims of sexual abuse are 4 times more likely to abuse drugs and experience PTSD.

Victims of sexual abuse are 3 times more likely to experience depression.

93% of victims know their perpetrator.

34% of perpetrators are family members.

Every 73 seconds, an American is sexually assaulted.

1 out of every 6 American women has been the victim of an attempted or completed rape in her lifetime.

1 in 33 men have experienced an attempted or completed rape in their lifetime.

The majority of sexual assaults occur at or near the victim's home.

38% of victims of sexual violence experience work or school problems.

37% experience family/friend problems, including getting into arguments more frequently and not feeling able to trust.

The number of children conceived from rape each year in the United States might range from 7,750 - 12,500.

Every 98 seconds, someone in the U.S. is sexually assaulted. That means that every day, 570 people experience sexual violence.

Tips for Handling Sexual Assault/Abuse

As a Victim: Tell someone what happened. Tell a parent, trusted friend, and/or the police. You don't have to be scared or ashamed. What happened is not your fault. Recovery is a process. It may take months or years to process what happened and heal from it. However long it takes, God can and will bring you through to victory on the other side.

As a Confidant: If someone decides to confide in you that they have been abused or assaulted, try your best to provide a safe space. Don't be judgmental or ask judgmental questions. The last thing that person needs is to feel judged. He or she is already experiencing a range of emotions that are likely overwhelming for them. Don't talk too much. Mainly be a listening ear and support. Ask the person what he or she needs from you.

Scriptures

The Word of God along with prayer are great tools for the transition from victim to victor. The following scriptures are for encouragement and healing. They serve as a reminder of who God is and who we are and were created to be in Him.

God's Plan and Purpose:

Jeremiah 1:5 - "Before I formed you in the womb I knew you, before you were born I set you apart; I appointed you as a prophet to the nations.

Jeremiah 29:11-14 - "For I know the plans I have for you," declares the Lord, "plans to prosper you and not to harm you, plans to give you a hope and a future. Then you will call on me and come and pray to me, and I will listen to you. You will seek me with all you heart. I will be found by you," declares the Lord, "and I will bring you back from captivity. I will gather you from all the nations and places where I have banished you," declares the Lord, "and will bring you back to the place from which I carried you into exile."

Proverbs 3:5-6 - "Trust in the Lord with all your heart and lean not on your own understanding; in all your ways submit to him, and he will make your paths straight."

Proverbs 16:9 - "In their hearts humans plan their course, but the Lord establishes their steps."

Proverbs 19:21 - "Many are the plans in a person's heart, but it is the Lord's purpose that prevails."

Psalm 57:2 - "I cry out to God Most High, to God, who vindicates me."

Psalm 62:8 - "Trust in him at all times, you people; pour out your hearts to him, for God is our refuge."

Philippians 4:19 - " And my God will meet all your needs according to the riches of his glory in Christ Jesus."

Isaiah 58:11 - "The Lord will guide you always; he will satisfy your needs in a sun - scorched land and will strengthen your frame. You will be like a well - watered garden, like a spring whose waters never fail."

Isaiah 41:10 - "So do not fear, for I am with you, do not be dismayed, for I am your God."

Matthew 11:28-30 - "Come to me, all you who are weary and burdened, and I will give you rest. Take my yoke upon you and learn from me, for I am gentle and humble in heart, and you will find rest for your souls. For my yoke is easy and my burden is light."

Psalm 139:13-14 - "For you created my inmost being, you knit me together in my mother's womb. I praise you because I am fearfully and wonderfully made; your works are wonderful, I know that full well."

Genesis 50:20 - "You intended to harm me, but God intended it for good to accomplish what is now being done, the saving of many lives."

God's Agape Love:

Agape - The highest form of love of God for man and of man for God.

John 3:16 - "For God so loved the world that he gave his one and only Son, that whoever believes in him shall not perish but have eternal life."

Romans 5:8 - "But God demonstrates his own love for us in this: While we were still sinners, Christ died for us."

Ephesians 3:17-19 - "So that Christ may dwell in your hearts through faith. And I pray that you, being rooted and established in love, may have power, together with all the Lord's holy people, to grasp how wide and long and high and deep is the love that surpasses knowledge- that you may be filled to the measure of all the fullness of God.

Lamentations 3:22-23 - "Because of the Lord's great love we are not consumed, for his compassions never fail. They are new every morning; great is your faithfulness."

Victory:

Deuteronomy 20:4 - "For the Lord your God is the one who goes with you to fight for you against your enemies to give you victory."

1 Corinthians 15:57 - But thanks be to God, which giveth us the victory through our Lord Jesus Christ."

Romans 8:37 - "No, in all these things we are more than conquerors through him who loved us."

Healing:

Psalm 30:2 - "Lord my God, I called to you for help, and you healed me.

Psalm 147:3 - "He heals the brokenhearted and binds up their wounds."

Psalm 107: 19-21 - "Then they cried to the Lord in their trouble, and he saved them from their distress. He sent out his word and healed them; he rescued them from the grave. Let them give thanks to the Lord for his unfailing love and his wonderful deeds for mankind."

Jeremiah 30:7 - "But I will restore you to health and heal your wounds, declares the Lord, because you are called an outcast, Zion for whom no one cares.

Philippians 4:19 - "And my God will meet all your needs according to the riches of his glory in Christ Jesus."

References

Salmona, Dr. Muriel. "Traumatic Amnesia: A Dissociative Survival Mechanism" www.memoiretraumatique.org, 2018.

Finch, Sam Dylan. "Five Ways I'm Unlearning My Fawn Response".

www.letsqueerthingsup.com, 2020.

Vagianos, Alanna. "Thirty Alarming Statistics That Show the Reality of Sexual Violence in America". www.huffpost.com, 2017.

RAINN (Rape, Abuse, and Incest National Network). www.rainn.org, 2021. The National Children's Advocacy Center. www.nationalcac.org, 2021.

The National Child Traumatic Stress Network. www.nctsn.org, 2021.

About the Author

Barbara Swint is an author and sexual abuse advocate. She is the founder of Still Standing LLC. She resides in Huntsville, AL with her daughter and three grandchildren.

For more information and booking, contact: imstillstanding-llc.org

www.ingramcontent.com/pod-product-compliance
Lightning Source LLC
Chambersburg PA
CBHW042128160426
43198CB00021B/2948